Money in Hand, Wisdom in Your Pocket

Financial Education for Young People

Marcelo da Silva Guerra

DEDICATION

I dedicate this book to all young people who dare to dream big, believing that knowledge is the key to achieving a bright future. To those who understand that financial wisdom is a superpower that allows them to shape their destiny, build their dreams, and tread a path of independence and success.

To young people who face financial challenges with courage, who seek personal growth and financial freedom, and who are determined to make every penny work in their favor.

May the pages of this book inspire you to achieve your goals, make conscious decisions, and walk the path to a more prosperous financial life.

Always remember: money may be in our hands, but true wealth lies in the wisdom we carry in our pockets.

CONTENT

PREFACE

In an ever-changing world, money is a powerful tool that can propel your dreams forward or become an overwhelming obstacle. For young people who are about to start their financial journeys, knowledge is truly the best investment. And that's where **"Money in Hand, Wisdom in Your Pocket"** comes into play.

This book is an engaging and practical guide, specially created for young people seeking financial independence. With an accessible and inspiring approach, you'll immerse yourself in a fascinating world of financial education, learning not only how to manage your money, but also how to make it work for you.

Find out how to create a budget that allows you to realize your dreams while keeping your finances in check. Learn to decipher the secrets of investing by exploring the opportunities that the financial market offers. Learn how to avoid the pitfalls of debt and impulsive consumption, and build a solid foundation for your financial future.

"Money in Hand, Wisdom in Your Pocket" is not just a guide, it is a companion on the journey. You'll be inspired to turn your dreams into reality through smart financial management. In addition, theoretical exercises will help you understand the concepts learned and set concrete financial goals.

Get ready for an educational adventure that will empower you to make decisions and achieve the financial freedom you deserve. This book is the compass that will guide you in the search for a bright financial future.

"Money in Hand, Wisdom in Your Pocket" is the key to unlocking your financial potential and shaping your own destiny.

Money in Hand, Wisdom in Your Pocket

Marcelo Guerra

1- Introduction to Financial Education

Financial education is critical for young people for a number of reasons as it provides crucial knowledge and skills to deal with the complexities of the financial world. Here are a few reasons why financial education is important for young people.

Decision-making

Financial decision-making is an important concept for teens to understand, as it refers to the choices we make about how to earn, spend, save, and invest our money. Through financial education, young people learn to make decisions. This includes the ability to evaluate credit, investment and spending options based on solid data and not just impulses.

Prevention of indebtedness

Debt prevention means taking steps to prevent the accumulation of unnecessary debt or spending more money than you can afford. This involves planning your finances, making smart spending choices, and adopting responsible financial habits. Understanding concepts such as interest, loans, and credit cards helps young people avoid excessive debt. This is essential to avoid financial pitfalls that could harm your economic future.

Development of budgeting skills

Financial education teaches young people how to create and maintain budgets. This skill helps ensure that they know how much they earn, how much they spend, and how to save to achieve financial goals.

Emergency preparedness
Life is full of financial surprises, such as unexpected medical expenses or job loss. Financial education teaches young people how to create emergency funds to deal with these situations without panicking.

Smart investments
Learning about investments, such as stocks, bonds, and real estate, can help young people increase their wealth over time. The sooner they start investing, the greater the growth potential of their assets.

Understanding the financial system
Financial education also provides information about how the financial system works, including banks, credit institutions, and investments. This makes young consumers more aware and able to make well-informed financial choices.

Financial empowerment
Financial education gives young people a sense of control over their own financial future. They become less dependent on third parties to make important financial decisions.

Reduction of financial stress
With financial knowledge, young people are less likely to constantly worry about money. This can significantly improve your quality of life and emotional well-being.

Building a solid future

By acquiring financial skills from an early age, young people have the opportunity to build a solid future, with the ability to achieve their long-term financial goals, such as buying a home, financing their children's education, or retiring.

Contributing to a more resilient society

Financially educated individuals are less likely to turn to government assistance or fall into debt traps, which can contribute to a stronger society economically.

In short.

Financial education is an essential tool to empower young people to make wise financial decisions and build a secure and prosperous financial future. It benefits not only individuals, but also society as a whole, by promoting economic stability and financial independence.

The book **"Money in Hand, Wisdom in Your Pocket"** has as main objectives:

Promote Financial Education
The book seeks to teach young people the fundamental principles of financial education, empowering them to make smart financial decisions throughout their lives.

Develop Healthy Financial Habits
One of the main goals is to help young people cultivate healthy financial habits such as saving, investing, avoiding unnecessary debt, and managing money effectively.

Preparing for the Future
The book aims to prepare young people for the financial challenges they will face throughout their lives, including the transition to adulthood, college, the job market and financial independence.

Stimulate Financial Planning
Encourages readers to create a personal financial plan that takes into account short- and long-term goals, such as buying a home, retirement, and investing.

Promotes Understanding of Finance
The book explores complex financial concepts in an accessible way, making them understandable to young people, such as interest, budgeting, investing, and diversification.

Avoid Financial Pitfalls
Warning young people about common financial pitfalls, such as irresponsible use of credit, impulsive spending, and a lack of savings, is another important goal of the book.

Encourage Financial Self-Confidence
By educating young people about personal finance, the book seeks to increase their self-confidence and ability to make financial decisions independently.

Promoting Financial Sustainability
The book includes information on the importance of financial sustainability, encouraging young people to adopt financial practices that help them maintain a healthy balance between current and future needs.

"Money in Hand, Wisdom in Your Pocket" seeks to empower young people with the skills and knowledge needed to achieve financial stability and make smart financial decisions throughout their lives.

How to use the book

"Money in Hand, Wisdom in Your Pocket" is a book that seeks to teach important principles of financial education in an accessible and practical way for young people. Here are some steps you can take to get the most out of this book.

Careful reading
Start by reading the book from start to finish. Make sure you understand the concepts presented in each chapter. Don't be in a hurry; absorb the contents gradually.

Notes
As you read, make notes of the concepts, tips, and strategies that catch your eye the most. This will help to consolidate knowledge.

Set your financial goals
One of the first important steps in financial education is to set clear goals. Use the book to help you understand how to set realistic and specific financial goals for your future.

Personal budget
Learn about the importance of creating and maintaining a personal budget. The book provides guidance on how to do this effectively. Start tracking your expenses and income.

Save and invest
Learn about different types of investments, such as stocks, bonds, and mutual funds. Find out how to save and invest your money according to your financial goals.

Debt and credit

Understand the associated risks and how to manage credit responsibly. The book covers strategies for avoiding common debt-related pitfalls.

Planning for emergencies

Make sure you understand how to prepare for financial emergencies, such as unexpected medical expenses or job loss. Having an emergency reserve is key.

Healthy financial habits

Use the book to identify and adopt healthy financial habits. This includes things like saving regularly, avoiding impulsive spending, and living within your means.

Consult a financial professional

If you have specific decisions or more complex financial plans, consider consulting with a financial professional.

Share with friends and family

Sharing financial knowledge with friends and family can be beneficial for everyone. You can learn together and support each other on your financial journeys.

Apply what you've learned

Financial education is not only about acquiring but also about applying that knowledge in real life. Put the lessons learned in the book into practice to improve your financial situation.

Periodic evaluation

Reread portions of the book and reassess your financial goals regularly. As your life changes, your financial goals can evolve.

"Money in Hand, Wisdom in Your Pocket" is a useful tool to help young people develop solid financial skills. Remember that financial education is an ongoing journey, and the book can be a helpful guide along that path.

Marcelo Guerra

2- Controlling Your Money

A budget is a plan you create to control your money. It's like a map that shows you how much money you have and where it goes. It's a smart way to manage your money so you can spend it consciously and reach your financial goals.

Revenue
This includes all the money you receive, such as pocket money, birthday money, or money you earn from temp jobs. It's important to know how much money you have available to spend.

Expenditure
It's all the things you spend money on, like snacks, clothes, hanging out with friends, and even saving for specific goals, like a video game. Write down all your expenses. Expenses can be classified into **Fixed and Variable.**

Fixed expenses
These are expenses that you have regularly every month and usually have a constant value. These expenses are predictable and don't change much from one month to the next.

Common examples of fixed expenses include rent, mortgage, utility bills (such as water, electricity, gas, and telephone), school or college tuition, and payment of a loan or mortgage. Even if you want to save, it's usually not easy reduce these expenses in the short term, as they are mandatory.

Variable expenses

These are expenses that can vary from month to month and usually depend on your choices and needs. These expenses do not have a fixed amount and can be adjusted based on situations. Examples of variable expenses include food, entertainment, clothing, transportation (such as fuel or public transportation), gifts, and leisure activities. You have more control over these expenses and can save money by adjusting your spending according to your budget.

Summarizing

The main difference between fixed expenses and variable expenses is that fixed expenses are regular, mandatory, and have consistent values, while variable expenses are more flexible, dependent on your choices, and can vary from month to month.

Difference

Subtract your expenses from your income. If the result is positive, it means that you are spending less than you earn, which is great. If it's negative, you're spending more than you earn, and that can be a problem.

Adjustment

If you find that you're spending more than you earn, you'll need to adjust your budget. This may involve reducing some expenses, finding ways to make more money (such as doing extra work), or saving for bigger goals.

Remember:

A budget helps you be responsible with your money, save for important things, and avoid unnecessary debt. It's an important skill that will help you manage your finances throughout your life.

BUDGET DOMESTIC

REVENUE	VALUE
Salary	
Extra income	
Gift	
Investment	
TOTAL	

FIXED EXPENSE	VALUE
Rent	
Condominium	
Taxes	
Transport	
School	
Academy	
Loan	
SUB TOTAL 1	

EXTRA EXPENSE	VALUE
Gifts	
Leisure	
Movie theater	
Sport	
Trip	
SUB TOTAL 2	

VARIABLE EXPENSE	VALUE
Light	
Water	
Bakery	
Butcher's	
Market	
SUB TOTAL 2	

TOTAL REVENUE	+	
SUB TOTAL 1	-	
SUB TOTAL 2	-	
SUB TOTAL 3	-	
BALANCE		

MARCH 2024

Exercises

1. What is a budget?
a) An identification document.
b) A shopping list for the month.
c) A plan that helps you manage your money.
d) A secret password for your online accounts.
e) A type of computer.

2. Why is it important to have a budget?
a) To make parents happy.
b) To know how much money you can borrow.
c) To control your spending and save money.
d) To avoid doing physical exercises.
e) Because it is a current fad.

3. What is the difference between "income" and "expense"?
a) Revenue you spend, expense you receive.
b) Revenue you receive, expense you spend.
c) Income and expenditure are the same thing.
d) Revenue and expenditure are not related to budget.
e) Revenue is for the adult, and expense is for the young person.

4. What is an "emergency fund"?
a) A place where you save money for vacations.
b) Save money to buy something expensive in the future.
c) Money set aside to cover unexpected expenses.
d) Save energy at home.
e) It is a type of safe.

5. How can you keep track of your budget?
a) Using a financial management application.
b) Asking your parents to do it for you.
c) It is not necessary to keep track of the money.
d) Spending all the money as soon as you receive it.
e) There is no way to keep up.

6. What are fixed expenses?
a) Expenses that change in value each month.
b) Expenses that you can spend or not to spend.
c) Expenses that have a constant value.
d) Expenses that only adults have.
e) Expenses that only young people have.

7. What alternative is an example of a fixed expense?
a) Buy a birthday present.
b) Pay the electricity bill every month.
c) Going to the movies with friends.
d) Eating out in a restaurant.
e) Buy new clothes.

8. What is specific to fixed expenditure?
a) They change in value every month.
b) They are indications, you can choose to spend or not.
c) They are unpredictable.
d) They are one-time expenses.
e) They are regular and have a constant value.

9. Which alternative is not a fixed expense?
a) School tuition.
b) Payment of a student loan.
c) Food from the supermarket.
d) Rent or mortgage.
e) Mobile phone bill.

10. Why is it important to know your fixed expenses?
a) Because you can spend as much as you want.
b) Because they are donations.
c) Because you need to plan your budget.
d) Because fixed expenses are paid by your parents.
e) Because you can ignore and spend your money.

11. What are variable expenses?
a) Expenses that are always the same every month.
b) Expenses that are optional.
c) Expenses that are required by law.
d) Expenses that are paid once a year.
e) Expenses that are determined by the parents.

12. Which of the alternatives is a variable expense?
a) Rent or mortgage.
b) School tuition.
c) Food from the supermarket.
d) Internet account.
e) Payment of a student loan.

13. What is specific to variable expenses?
a) They are always the same every month.
b) They are compulsory expenditure.
c) They are predictable and have a constant value.
d) They depend on your choices and needs.
e) They are paid only once in a lifetime.

14. Which of the alternatives is not a variable expense?
a) New clothes.
b) Water bill.
c) Dinner out with friends.
d) Buy birthday gifts.
e) Go to the grocery.

15. Why is it important to control variable expenses?
a) Because they are always the same every month.
b) Because you have no control over them.
c) because they are compulsory expenditure.
d) Because you can adjust your spending.
e) Because they are determined by the parents.

Answers

1) c
2) c
3) b
4) c
5) a
6) c
7) b
8) e
9) c
10) c
11) b
12) c
13) d
14) b
15) d

Marcelo Guerra

3- Ways to Save Money

Saving money is an important skill that all teens can learn. Even with a limited allowance or money you earn occasionally, it's possible to adopt healthy financial habits from an early age. Here are some simple tips to help you save money.

Set Financial Goals

Start by setting clear goals for what you want to save. It could be to buy a video game, a new cell phone, or to have an emergency fund. Having goals makes it easier to motivate yourself to save.

Create a Budget

As mentioned earlier, a budget is key. Write down all your income (allowance, birthday present, temporary jobs) and then list your expenses. This will help you understand where your money is going and where you can save.

Prioritize Spending

Evaluate your expenses and determine what is essential and what is superfluous. Prioritize the important things and cut out unnecessary expenses, such as snacking or impulsive shopping.

Avoid Debt

Avoid using credit cards unless absolutely necessary. Debts can be difficult to pay off and can cost more money in the long run due to interest.

Save regularly

Set aside a portion of your income to save as soon as you receive it. This can be a fixed percentage, like 10% of everything you earn. Put that money into a savings account.

Buy wisely

When shopping, research prices, compare offers, and avoid impulse buying. Ask yourself if the item is really needed and if you can find a cheaper alternative.

Take advantage of Offers and Discounts

Use coupons, take advantage of promotions and discounts whenever possible. This can save you a lot of money over time.

Be Disciplined

Remember that saving money requires discipline. Avoid spending all your money as soon as you receive it and remember your financial goals.

Learn About Investing

As you accumulate more money, consider learning about low-risk investments such as savings accounts or bonds. This can help your money grow over time.

Ask for Advice

Don't be afraid to ask your parents or responsible adults for financial advice. They can offer valuable guidance to help you save and manage your money successfully.

Remember:

Saving money is a skill that improves over time. The sooner you start practicing these financial habits, the more prepared you'll be to deal with your finances in the future. It can be challenging at first, but the long-term benefits of being financially responsible are invaluable.

Exercises

1. What is the first step to saving money?
a) Set financial goals.
b) Spend all the money you have.
c) Ignore your expenses.
d) Borrow money.
e) Stop working.

2. What is a budget?
a) A shopping list.
b) A way to make extra money.
c) A plan to control revenue and expenditure.
d) A raffle.
e) A board game.

3. Why is it important to avoid impulse purchases?
a) Impulse purchases are always a good idea.
b) Because they can lead to unnecessary expenses.
c) Because all the friends are doing it.
d) Because my father spoke.
e) Because it's fashion.

4. What can help save money?
a) Buy by credit card.
b) Buy the first item you see.
c) Spend as much as possible.
d) Compare prices, promotions and ask for discounts.
e) Buy by check.

5. What does it mean to "live within your means"?
a) Spend more money than you earn.
b) Spend only what you can afford.
c) Do not spend money.
d) Stop working.
e) Stop studying.

6. How important is it to save money?
a) It is not important to save.
b) It is important to borrow money.
c) It is important to spend all the money immediately.
d) This helps to increase expenses.
e) This helps to create an emergency fund.

7. How can you avoid spending on snacks and food?
a) Take snacks from home and cook meals at home.
b) Eat in restaurants every day.
c) Ignore your hunger.
d) Not eating.
e) Eat only French fries every day.

8. What is the way to take advantage discounts?
a) Never pay attention to discounts.
b) Buy the first item you see.
c) Use coupons and compare prices before buying.
d) It is better to stay at home.
e) Impulse buying.

9. What can you do with saved money?
a) Spend it immediately on things you want.
b) It is better to leave it stored forever.
c) Donate it to charity.
d) Spend with friends.
e) Keep it in a savings account.

10. Why is it important to learn about personal finance from an early age?
a) It is not important.
b) I don't know why; I just know it's important.
c) Because other people will take care of your money.
d) To develop financial skills.
e) Because my mother spoke.

11. How can I save money?
a) Spend all the money you earn.
b) Buy luxury items regularly.
c) Make impulse purchases without planning.
d) Create a budget and track your spending.
e) Completely ignore your finances.

12. Which alternative saves energy and money?
a) All lights on all the time.
b) The electronic devices on.
c) Turn off the lights when not in use.
d) Wash clothes several times a day.
e) The faucet open while brushing your teeth.

Answers

1) a
2) c
3) b
4) d
5) b
6) e
7) a
8) c
9) e
10) d
11) d
12) c

Marcelo Guerra

4- Checking Account

A checking account is a bank account that you can use to store money, make deposits, withdrawals, pay bills, and receive your salary. It's called "checking account" because you can easily access your money at any time, whether it's through checks, debit cards, ATMs, or online transactions.

Why Open a Checking Account?

Financial Management
A checking account offers an organized way to manage your money. You can see how much money you have, track your spending, and even set up alerts to monitor your transactions.

Receive Payments
If you have a job or trainee, a checking account allows your salary to be deposited directly into your account. This is convenient and safe.

Pay bills
With a checking account, you can pay your own bills, such as the mobile plan or even contribute to household expenses.

Debit Card
Most checking accounts come with a debit card that allows you to make purchases in physical stores and online, making it a safer alternative to cash.

Using Your Current Account Responsibly

Keep Records
Write down your transactions to keep track of your spending.
This helps to avoid unpleasant surprises on the bank statement.

Avoid Fees
Check the bank's policies on maintenance fees or other fees. Many banks offer free checking accounts for teens.

Protect your card
Keep your debit card safe and don't share your password with strangers.

Pay bills on time
If you're using your checking account to pay bills, be sure to do so on time to avoid penalties.

Save money
Consider creating savings for long-term goals. Saving is a key part of personal finances.

Conclusion
Opening a checking account is an important step in learning how to manage your finances. It is a tool that offers convenience and financial responsibility. With proper care and attention to your finances, your checking account can be a valuable tool as you grow and mature financially. Remember that knowledge and responsible practice are essential for a healthy financial life.

Exercises

1. What is a checking account?
a) Type of savings exclusively for children.
b) Account that allows the withdrawal of money.
c) Account used only for investments in shares.
d) Retirement account.
e) Type of investment.

2. What is the main difference between a checking account and a savings account?
a) Savings account has a food card.
b) Savings account you earn interest on your balance.
c) Current account is intended for adults only.
d) Savings account is used only to pay bills.
e) Current account you earn interest on your balance.

3. What can you do with a checking account?
a) Receive salary and pay bills.
b) Pay only bills.
c) Receive interest on the balance.
d) Buy shares on the stock exchange.
e) Receive only salary.

4. Why is it important to keep a record of your transactions in a checking account?
a) To impress your friends.
b) To prevent your parents from seeing what you spend.
c) To track your income and expenses.
d) To have a record for income tax.
e) To improve your memory.

5. Why is it better to choose a bank with a low rate?
a) To obtain a credit card.
b) To earn interest on the account balance.
c) To avoid maintenance charges.
d) To have access to exclusive ATMs.
e) To show friends.

6. What is a bank statement?
a) A document that lists all online purchases.
b) A summary of the transactions.
c) An application for a new credit card.
d) A record of the shares the stock exchange.
e) An application to make bank transfers.

7. What else is possible to have in a checking account?
a) Collector's items, such as Pokémon cards.
b) Home furnishings.
c) A valid passport.
d) A debit card and/or a cheque book.
e) New clothes.

8. Which item is not associated with a checking account?
a) An account number.
b) A password.
c) A bank statement.
d) A cheque book.
e) A rent contract.

9. What is a bank slip?
a) A document for online shopping.
b) A credit card.
c) A document a bill to be paid.
d) A ticket for sporting events.
e) A gaming app.

10. What is the maturity in a bank slip for?
a) To remember someone's birthday.
b) To indicate the number of the document.
c) To show the address of the bank.
d) To set the deadline until the bill must be paid.
e) To show the customer's name.

11. How can you pay a bank slip?
a) Only in a physical store.
b) Only in cash.
c) In a bank, ATM or over the internet.
d) Calling the company that issued the slip.
e) It is not possible to pay bank slips.

12. What happens if you pay a slip after the due date?
a) Nothing happens, you can pay whenever you want.
b) The company issues another slip with a new date.
c) You need to pay a fine and interest.
d) The value of the slip is canceled.
e) The company cancels the account.

13. What is the importance of keeping the proof of payment of a bank slip?
a) To use as wallpaper on mobile.
b) It's not important, you can throw it away.
c) It is useful only to show to friends.
d) To prove that the bill has been paid.
e) To show to the bank manager.

Answers

1) b
2) b
3) a
4) c
5) c
6) b
7) d
8) e
9) c
10) d
11) c
12) c
13) d

Marcelo Guerra

5- Savings Account

Adolescence is an exciting phase of life, full of discoveries and new experiences. As you grow, it's also important to learn about personal finance, and one of the simplest ways to do this is to open a savings account. In this guide, we'll explore what a savings account is, why it's useful, and how you can get the most out of it.

What is a Savings Account?
A savings account is a bank account designed specifically to help people save money. Unlike a checking account, which is primarily used for daily transactions, a savings account is meant to save money in the long run. It offers a safe and effective way to save money and earn interest on the amount deposited.

Why open a Savings Account?

Save for Goals
A savings account is a great way to save for short- and long-term goals, such as buying a car, traveling, or paying for college.

Learn to Manage Finances
Opening a savings account can be an opportunity to learn about financial management. You can set savings goals, create a budget, and learn how to track your financial progress.

Earn Interest

All savings accounts pay interest on the deposited balance. This means that your money will grow over time, even without making large additional deposits.

Financial Security

Having a reserve in a savings account can help provide financial security in case of emergencies, such as unexpected medical expenses or home repairs.

Using Your Savings Account Responsibly

Set Savings Goals
Set clear goals for your financial goals. This will help you stay focused and efficient to save.

Regular Deposits
Try to make regular deposits into your savings account, even if they are small. The habit of saving regularly is critical to financial success.

Avoid Impulsive Withdrawals
Avoid withdrawing money from your savings account for unplanned spending. Maintain a discipline to achieve your savings goals.

Compare Interest Rates
Check the interest rates offered by different banks, to find the savings account that offers the best earnings.

Learn about Finance
Keep learning about personal finance, investing, and how to grow your money over time.

Conclusion
Opening a savings account is a smart step to building a solid financial foundation. It helps cultivate the habit of saving, offers financial security, and allows you to achieve your financial goals in the future. Remember that the key to a successful savings account is consistency, discipline, and understanding of how money can work in your favor over time. Starting to save early is an important step toward a financially stable and prosperous future.

Exercises

1. What is a savings account?
a) Account to pay only the monthly expenses.
b) Account used exclusively to make a profit.
c) Account designed to hold money and earn interest.
d) Account only for online shopping.
e) Account to receive a card and show it to friends.

2. What is the main feature of the savings account?
a) Ability to make credit card purchases.
b) Earn interest on the money stored in the account.
c) Receive a salary directly in the account.
d) Withdraw money at any time.
e) Deposit money at any time.

3. Why is it important to set financial goals when opening a savings account?
a) To make purchases without restrictions.
b) To lose money with interest.
c) To lose the money saved in the long run.
d) To have a clear goal to save.
e) To show to parents.

4. What is the best way to use the savings account?
a) Spend all the money you earn quickly.
b) Withdraw money regularly.
c) Accumulating money with deposits and interest.
d) Invest in shares on the stock exchange.
e) Make purchases with a credit card.

5. What does "interest" mean in a savings account?
a) Fee you pay to the bank.
b) Exchange rate.
c) Fee you receive from the bank.
d) Fee for transferring the money.
e) Fee for depositing the money.

6. What happens if I withdraw money from the savings account?
a) You get more interest.
b) You cannot withdraw money from the savings account.
c) You pay less bank fees.
d) Your interest earnings are lower.
e) You get discounts on purchases.

7. What is the minimum age to open a savings account?
a) 21 years.
b) 18 years.
c) 16 years.
d) 13 years.
e) 10 years.

Answers

1) c
2) b
3) d
4) c
5) c
6) d
7) b

Note: The minimum age to open a savings account at most banks varies by financial institution and country, but is usually 18. However, many banks also offer savings accounts for minors, often from the age of 13, as long as the holder is assisted or authorized by a legal guardian, such as a parent or guardian. It is important to check the specific policies of the bank in question, as they may vary.

Marcelo Guerra

6- Checkbook

Checkbook is a set of sheets of paper issued by a bank so that customers can make payments from their bank account to other people or businesses. Each sheet of the checkbook contains important information, such as the name of the account holder, the bank account number, and the check identification number. Here is some basic information about checkbooks.

What is a checkbook?
A checkbook is a way to pay bills or make purchases using your bank account. It is an alternative to cash and credit/debit cards.

How does it work?
When you fill out a check, you write the amount you want to pay, the recipient's name, the location, and the date. Then you sign the check and a person or company that receives it can deposit it into their own bank account to receive the money.

Safety and Responsibility
It is important to treat the checkbook carefully as it is directly linked to your bank account. Keep it in a safe place and never share personal or contact information with strangers.

Records
Remember to keep a record of all the checks you issue, writing down the check number, recipients, and amount. This will help control and prevent overspending.

Fees and Limitations
Some banks charge fees for checkbooks or for each check issued. Also, keep in mind that checks have a limit on the funds available in your account. Issuing unfunded checks can result in additional fees and financial problems.

Conscious Use
Use checkbook responsibly and only when necessary. Many transactions can be done electronically, which can be more convenient and secure.

Keep in mind that in many parts of the world, the use of checks is being discontinued as electronic transactions become more popular.

Exercises

1. What is a checkbook?
a) A credit card.
b) A bank document to make payments.
c) An identity document.
d) A form of cash.
e) A public service bill.

2. What do you use a checkbook for?
a) To purchase items online.
b) To apply for a loan.
c) To make payments using your bank account.
d) To buy shares on the stock exchange.
e) To apply for a new credit card.

3. What should you include when filling out a check?
a) Only the name of the consignee.
b) The date only.
c) Your signature only.
d) The value, the name of the consignee and the date.
e) Only the bank account number of the consignee.

4. What happens when a cheque is issued without funds?
a) The bank will give you more money.
b) Nothing, the check will be paid anyway.
c) You will be fined and will have to pay additional fees.
d) The bank will cancel your bank account.
e) The recipient of the cheque will have to pay the fees.

5. What is safer when paying bills?
a) Use a debit card.
b) Issue a blank cheque.
c) Pay in cash.
d) Divide the amount into several checks.
e) Keep the money at home.

6. What should you do when issuing a check?
a) Disclose your bank details on social networks.
b) Keep the checkbook in a public place.
c) Write down the cheque number, recipient and value.
d) Use blank checks for all transactions.
e) Ignore the signature on the check.

Answers

1) b
2) c
3) d
4) c
5) a
6) c

Marcelo Guerra

7- Debit Card

D ebit card is a financial tool that allows you to spend money directly from your bank account. Here is some important information about the debit card.

Bank account access
When you own a debit card, it is conditioned on your bank account. This means that you can use the money that is in your account to make purchases or withdraw money at ATMs.

Cashless purchases
With a debit card, you can make purchases without needing physical cash. Simply insert the card into a payment machine (such as in a supermarket) or use it to shop online.

Personal Identification Number (PIN)
To make purchases with a debit card, you'll usually need to enter a secret number. It's important to keep this number safe and not share it with anyone.

Expense control
The debit card can help you control your spending as all transactions are recorded in your bank account. This allows you to keep track of how much you're spending and avoid spending more than you can.

Spending limits
Some debit cards may have daily or weekly spending limits. Know these limits to make sure you avoid problems.

Taxes and fees

It is important to know if your bank charges any fees for using the debit card. Many banks offer free debit cards to their customers, but it's good to check this out.

Safety

In case of loss or theft of the debit card, it is essential to contact the bank immediately to block it and prevent unauthorized use.

Responsible use

Remember that a debit card is directly related to your money. Use it responsibly and don't spend more than you can afford.

Benefits

Some debit cards offer benefits, such as rewards programs or discounts on purchases. Check if your card offers any kind of advantage.

Financial education

Having a debit card can be an opportunity to learn about financial management and budgeting. It's a practical way to understand how money and financial transactions work.

Remembering that a debit card is different from a credit card. With a debit card, you spend the money you already have in your account, while with a credit card you make purchases with a credit limit and need to pay the bill later. Therefore, it is important to understand the differences and use these financial tools responsibly.

Exercises

1. What is a debit card?
a) A card used for online games.
b) A card to spend money from your bank account.
c) A card granting loans for purchases.
d) A personal identification card.
e) A card just to withdraw money.

2. The PIN in relation to a debit card?
a) A barcode on the card.
b) The name of the bank which issued the card.
c) A shopping list made with the card.
d) A secret number.
e) A photo of the cardholder.

3. What is the main advantage of a debit card?
a) Make purchases without having money in the account.
b) Offers credit for future purchases.
c) Possibility to withdraw money at an ATM.
d) Allows you to earn reward points.
e) Automatically control your budget.

4. What to do if you lose your debit card?
a) Nothing, no one can use the card without the PIN.
b) Share the news on social networks.
c) Contact the bank to block the card.
d) Wait a few days to see if the card is returned.
e) Make a letter to the bank.

5. What is important when using a debit card?
a) It is not necessary to control spending.
b) Share the PIN with close friends.
c) Use the card to make personal loans.
d) Avoid spending more money than you have.
e) Store the card in a public place.

6. What can debit cards offer?
a) Free travel.
b) Discount coupon in restaurants.
c) Rewards programs and discounts on purchases.
d) Personal financial advice.
e) Access to exclusive sporting events.

7. To buy with a debit card, do you need to?
a) Enter the card number and your e-mail address.
b) Present a photo ID.
c) Enter the barcode of the product.
d) Insert the card and enter the PIN.
e) Send a check to the seller.

8. What is FedNow?
a) A form of payment with credit cards.
b) A social networking application.
c) A money transfer platform.
d) A popular video game.
e) A new species of bird.

9. Does the FedNow only work during business hours?
a) Yes, only from Monday to Friday.
b) No, 24 hours a day, every day of the week.
c) Yes, only from 9am to 5pm.
d) No, only at night.
e) Only on public holidays.

10. What is the FedNow for?
a) To make purchases in physical stores.
b) Only to pay electricity and water bills.
c) To transfer money and pay bills instantly.
d) To play online video games.
e) To order food in restaurants.

Answers

1) b
2) d
3) c
4) c
5) d
6) c
7) d
8) c
9) b
10) c

Marcelo Guerra

8- Credit Card

Credit cards can be a powerful financial tool, but they can also be a trap if not used responsibly. For teens who are just starting to learn about finance, a credit card can be an important introduction to the world of financial transactions. However, it is crucial to understand how to use it wisely. In this guide, we will discuss the responsible use of credit cards.

Basic Comprehension

A credit card is essentially a temporary loan you make from the bank or financial institution issuing the card. You can spend up to a predetermined credit limit, and at the end of the month, you must pay for what you spent. If you do not pay the full amount, you will have to pay interest on the unpaid balance.

Credit Construction

The first credit card is an opportunity to start building a credit history. Having a good credit history can be important in the future to get loans for the purchase of cars or houses. Paying your credit card bills on time helps build a positive credit history.

Set a Budget

Before using your credit card, it's important to establish a monthly budget. Determine how much money you can safely spend and avoid exceeding this limit. A credit card is not a license to spend without limits.

Pay the Balance in Full
The rule of thumb with credit cards is to pay off the balance in full each month. This will prevent the accumulation of interest. If you pay only the minimum amount, you will pay significant interest and take much longer to pay off your debt.

Avoid unnecessary debt
Use your credit card responsibly. Don't use it to buy superfluous items or things you can't afford. Resist the temptation to accumulate debt, as this can become a significant financial burden.

Control Your Spending
Keep a record of all your credit card spending. This will help you understand where your money is going and avoid impulsive spending.

Stay Tuned for Fees
Read your credit card terms and conditions carefully. Be aware of the interest rates, annual fees, and any other fees associated with your card.

Security is Fundamental
Keep your credit card safe. Never share your card number, PIN, or personal information with strangers. If you lose the card, immediately notify the issuing company to prevent misuse.

In brief

A credit card can be a useful tool, but it's important to use it responsibly. Learning to control your finances from an early age is a valuable skill that will accompany you throughout life. If used wisely, a credit card can be a tool for building a solid financial future. So stick to a budget, pay off your balance in full, and avoid unnecessary debt to make the most of your credit card benefits.

.

Exercises

1. What is a credit card?
a) A form of personal identification.
b) A card that allows you to make purchases online.
c) A means of payment using borrowed money.
d) A card only for ATM withdrawals.
e) A way to show off to friends.

2. What is the difference between credit and debit card?
a) Credit card is issued only by banks.
b) Credit card allows you to spend borrowed money.
c) Debit card has a high spending limit.
d) Credit card withdraws money from the account.
e) There is no difference between them.

3. What is a credit card's credit limit?
a) Amount you must pay each month.
b) Maximum amount you can spend with the card.
c) Interest you pay on the card balance.
d) Number of months you can use the card.
e) Numbers of months you do not pay interest.

4. What is the Annual Interest Rate on the credit card?
a) Amount of money you can spend.
b) Fee that is charged on the unpaid balance on the card.
c) Monthly maturity data of the card.
d) exchange rate.
e) Fee you receive for leaving the money on the card.

5. Why is it important to pay the full amount of the credit card each month?
a) To accumulate reward points.
b) To improve the credit limit.
c) To avoid interest on the unpaid balance.
d) To receive credit card offers.
e) To help the bank manager.

6. What is a credit card bill?
a) A receipt you receive when you make a purchase.
b) A notice about the interest rate of the card.
c) A statement monthly and the amount payable.
d) A document to withdraw money.
e) A proof of balance available on the card.

Answers

1) c
2) b
3) b
4) b
5) c
6) c

Marcelo Guerra

9- Compound Interest

I magine that you have some money saved, such as pocket money or a birthday present, and you decide to put it in a savings account at the bank. The bank, in return, pays a small amount of extra money for you to leave your money there. This extra money is called **interest**.

Now, there are two main types of interest: **simple** and **compound.** Let's focus on compound interest.

Compound interest
They're like a snowball that's going to get bigger as it rolls down the mountain. What this means is that, unlike simple interest, where you earn interest only on the initial amount you invested, in compound interest, you earn interest on the initial amount and also on the interest you have already earned previously.

Let's use a simple example to illustrate this:

Suppose you put $100 in your savings account and the bank pays 5% compound interest per year. In the first year, you will earn $5 (5% of $100). Now, you have $105 in the account. In the second year, you will earn 5% of $105, which is $5.25. Now you have $110.25 in the account.

This process continues each year, and your earnings increase because you are earning interest not only on the initial amount, but also on the interest you have already earned.

That's what makes compound interest so powerful. They help your money grow faster over time, as long as you keep keeping it in the savings account.

So, to summarize:
Compound interest is like a snowball that grows as time goes on, making your money grow more effectively.

Exercises

1. What is compound interest?
a) Interest paid only once a year.
b) Interest paid every day.
c) Interest paid at the beginning of an investment.
d) Interest paid in the initial amount and in the accrued interest.
e) Interest paid from time to time.

2. Suppose you invest $500 in a savings account that pays 3% compound interest per year. How much money will you have after 2 years?
a) $515
b) $530
c) $520.50
d) $510
e) $530.45

3. What is the difference between simple and compound interest?
a) Compound interest is paid in cash, while simple interest is paid in products.
b) Compound interest is paid only once a year, while simple interest is paid every month.
c) Compound interest is paid on the initial amount and also on the interest already accrued, while simple interest is paid only on the initial value.
d) Compound interest is payments only on loans, while simple interest is payments on investments.
e) Compound interest is for adults, while simple interest is for teenagers.

4. Why is compound interest considered more powerful over time?
a) They are simpler to calculate.
b) Are paid more frequently.
c) This is interest not only on the initial amount, but also on the interest already received.
d) They are used only in large investments.
e) They are paid only once.

5. If you let a compound interest investment grow for a long period of time, what will happen to your money?
a) Decrease.
b) Equal to the initial value.
c) It will increase steadily, but not by much.
d) It will increase a lot, due to compound interest.
e) It depends on the bank manager.

Answers

1) d
2) e
3) c
4) c
5) d

Marcelo Guerra

10- Emergency Fund

An emergency fund is a financial reserve that is intended for the purpose of helping to deal with unexpected expenses or emergencies that may arise in life. Even though teens generally don't have as many financial responsibilities as adults, it's important to learn early on the importance of having money in store. Here are some key points about what an emergency fund is.

Security Purpose
The emergency fund is designed to provide financial security in unexpected situations, such as medical expenses, vehicle or electronics repairs, or any other financial emergency.

Regular Economy
To build an emergency fund, a teenager must set aside a regular portion of their money (allowance, income from a part-time job, etc.) and direct it to that fund. This helps to create a savings from an early age.

Recommended amount
While there is no fixed amount, many experts recommend saving at least three to six times the amount of your monthly expenses. However, for a teenager, it may be more realistic to start with a smaller dimension and increase it gradually.

Savings Account
It is advisable to keep the emergency fund in a savings account, preferably in a bank, where money can be easily accessed when needed, but not so accessible as to spend it impulsively.

Not for Routine Spending
It is important to emphasize that the emergency fund should not be used for routine spending or impulse purchases. It should be reserved for legitimate financial emergencies.

Financial Education
Establishing and maintaining an emergency fund is also a valuable opportunity to teach teens financial skills such as budgeting, saving, and long-term planning.

Self-Reliance Goal
The ultimate goal is that when the adolescent becomes an adult, he or she will be able to handle financial emergencies without relying on parents or guardians.

Having an emergency fund can provide peace of mind and a sense of security, even for teens, and prepare them to face financial challenges more effectively as they grow up. It's a valuable lesson about financial responsibility that can benefit you throughout your life.

Exercises

1. What is an emergency fund?
a) High-risk investment fund.
b) Savings fund to buy luxury items.
c) Financial reserve for unexpected expenses.
d) Bank account for daily expenses.
e) Fund to finance holiday travel.

2. Why is it important to have an emergency fund?
a) To spend on impulsive purchases.
b) To show friends.
c) To help build a credit history.
d) For financial security in unexpected situations.
e) To buy expensive fashion items.

3. What is the value for an emergency fund?
a) One time the amount of the expenses.
b) At least 10 times the amount of the expenses.
c) At least 3 to 6 times the amount of the expenses.
d) The money left over at the end of the month.
e) It is not necessary to have an emergency fund.

4. Where is it advisable to keep an emergency fund?
a) In a savings account.
b) In a current account.
c) In a wallet.
d) In high-risk stocks and bonds.
e) In a piggy bank.

5. What is the goal of having an emergency fund?
a) To spend on entertainment.
b) To buy designer clothes.
c) Financial dependence on parents.
d) To dealing with financial emergencies.
e) To finance luxury travel.

6. When should the emergency fund be used?
a) To buy of new clothe.
b) Entertainment spending.
c) Regular expenses, such as rent and monthly bills.
d) Luxury holiday expenses.
e) Unexpected repairs at home or in the car.

Answers

1) c
2) d
3) c
4) a
5) d
6) e

Marcelo Guerra

11- Living Within Your Means

Living within your means" is a financial principle that means managing your money responsibly, ensuring that you spend only what you can afford based on your current income and avoid going into unnecessary debt. For a teenager, this entails several important actions and attitudes.

Budget
Creating a personal budget is the first step. This involves listing all sources of income, such as allowance, part-time work, etc., and then planning how you're going to spend that money.

Priorities
It is important to understand that money is finite. You should prioritize what is really important to you. This means distinguishing between your needs (such as food, transportation, and clothing) and desires (such as electronics, designer clothes).

Save money
Setting aside a portion of your income to save is crucial. This can be for short-term goals, such as a new video game, or long-term goals, such as a car or college.

Avoid debt
Avoid using credit cards or loans unless absolutely necessary. Debts can accumulate quickly and create a difficult financial situation.

Research before you buy
Before you spend money on something, research and compare prices. Often, you can find similar products for lower prices.

Being frugal
That means being economical and careful with money. It may involve things like buying generic products instead of expensive brands or reducing superfluous expenses.

Long-term planning
Think about the future. You may want to save for a college, a car, or a trip. Starting to plan now can make a big difference later.

Learning from mistakes
Everyone makes financial mistakes from time to time. The important thing is to learn from them and adjust your financial behavior to avoid repeating them.

Living within your means as a teenager doesn't mean you can't spend money on things you enjoy, but rather that you should do so consciously and responsibly, considering your financial limitations and thinking about your financial future. This is an important habit that will help build a solid foundation for a healthy financial life as you grow.

Exercises

1. What does it mean to "live within your means"?
a) Spend all the money.
b) Spend more money than you earn.
c) Spend only what you can afford.
d) Don't worry about money.
e) It means nothing.

2. Why is it important to create a budget?
a) To spend money impulsively.
b) To ensure that you never save.
c) To plan how you will spend your money.
d) To avoid making more money.
e) To lose money easier.

3. What are "needs"?
a) Things you want but don't need.
b) Things essential for their survival.
c) Money that you can spend freely.
d) Things you can borrow.
e) Things you can rent.

4. What is the most effective way to save money?
a) Spend all your money as soon as you receive it.
b) Avoid doing any kind of financial planning.
c) Keep a portion of your income.
d) Buy everything you want.
e) Buy gifts for friends.

5. Why is it important to avoid unnecessary debt?
a) Because debts are a way to get what you want.
b) Because debts can accumulate quickly.
c) Because debts do not affect your financial situation.
d) Because debts are good for improving credit.
e) The more debt, the better.

6. What is an example of living within your means?
a) Buying a large and expensive house with no money.
b) Save money to achieve financial goals.
c) Make loans to buy luxury items.
d) Ignore the budget and spend money without control.
e) Spend all the money as soon as you receive it.

Answers

1) c
2) c
3) b
4) c
5) b
6) b

Marcelo Guerra

12- Inflation

Inflation is a "general increase in prices." Imagine that you spend a certain amount to buy your favorite things, such as a hamburger, a pair of sneakers, or a video game.

Now, imagine that over time, the price of these things starts to rise gradually, which means that you need to spend more money to buy the same things that once cost less. That's **inflation.**

Inflation is an economic trend that occurs when the average price of the products and services we buy increases over time. In other words, it's as if the value of the money we have decreases because we can't buy the same amount of things with the same amount of money.

There are several reasons for inflation to occur. One is when the government prints more money, making it less valuable, and as a result, prices rise. Another reason may be the increase in production costs for companies, causing them to pass on these costs to consumers through higher prices.

Inflation can affect people's lives in many ways. For example, if prices rise too quickly, the power of your money decreases, which means you need to spend more to maintain the same standard of living. This can be especially challenging for people who have a tight budget.

Economists and governments follow inflation closely to ensure it doesn't get decontrol, as too high inflation can be detrimental to the economy. On the other hand, moderate inflation (a slower price increase) is considered normal in a healthy economy.

In short, inflation is the overall increase in prices over time, which can affect your money and your ability to buy the things you like. It is important to understand inflation to make financial decisions.

Exercises

1. What is inflation?
a) An increase in the number of products on the market.
b) Reduction in product prices over time.
c) A general increase in product prices.
d) Increase in the purchasing power of money.
e) Change in the season.

2. What can cause inflation?
a) Decrease in the money.
b) Reduction of production costs.
c) Increase in the purchasing power of money.
d) Increased production costs.
e) Reduction in demand for products.

3. How does inflation affect people's purchasing power?
a) Increases purchasing power.
b) Has no impact on purchasing power.
c) Decreases purchasing power.
d) It makes money more valuable.
e) Facilitates the purchase of products.

4. Why do governments follow inflation?
a) To increase the prices of products.
b) To guarantee the purchasing power of money.
c) To intentionally cause inflation.
d) To reduce the money.
e) To reduce the cost of production.

5. What is considered moderate inflation?
a) A very rapid increase in prices.
b) A slow increase in prices.
c) A decrease in prices.
d) A change in the seasons.
e) An exaggerated increase in prices.

6. What happens to the price in the period of inflation?
a) They remained unchanged.
b) They diminish.
c) They increase.
d) They become free.
e) They are prohibited.

Answers

1) c
2) d
3) c
4) b
5) b
6) c

Marcelo Guerra

13- Investing for the Long Term

Investing long-term is a key financial strategy, and that's for several important reasons.

Heritage Growth
Investing long-term allows money to grow over time due to the power of compound interest. The sooner you start investing, the more time your money will have to grow and multiply.

Preparing for the Future
As teens become adults, they face major expenses such as college, buying a car, and buying a home. Investing in the long term helps you accumulate the financial resources needed to face these expenses more smoothly.

Building Healthy Financial Habits
Learning to invest from an early age teaches teens about the importance of financial planning, discipline, and spending control. These are valuable habits that will help them make smarter financial decisions throughout their lives.

Risk Mitigation
Investing long-term allows you to diversify your investments, thereby decreasing financial risk. As time goes on, the ups and downs of the market have less impact on your portfolio, making it more resilient to economic downturns.

Seizing Time to Your Advantage

The most powerful factor of long-term investments is time. Starting to invest in your teens allows you to make the most of the time to increase your wealth. Small, regular investments can transform significantly over several decades.

Financial Independence

Investing long-term is an important step toward financial independence. This means that as you get older, you'll have the ability to make financial decisions based on your personal goals and values, rather than relying solely on negotiations or debt.

Continuous Learning

Investing is a field that requires continuous learning. Starting to invest early allows teens to acquire important financial knowledge and develop the ability to make investment decisions over time.

Adapting to Economic Change

Long-term investing also teaches you the importance of adapting your investment strategy to changing economic and evolving market conditions. This helps build lifelong financial resilience.

In summary:

Investing long-term is an effective way to build wealth, achieve important financial goals, and develop solid financial skills. Starting early offers a unique advantage due to the power of time and the potential for your money to grow over the decades. Therefore, it is highly recommended that teens start investing as early as possible, even if it is with small amounts, to reap the long-term benefits.

Exercises

1. Why is it important to invest long-term?
a) To make money quickly.
b) To accumulate debts.
c) To build a heritage over time.
d) To spend all the money immediately.
e) To buy luxury goods.

2. What is the main advantage of investing while still a teenager?
a) Increased financial risk.
b) Less time for money to grow.
c) Development of financial habits.
d) Fewer investment opportunities.
e) Greater dependence on loans.

3. What is compound interest?
a) A fixed rate of interest.
b) A variable interest rate.
c) Interest calculated only once a year.
d) Interest on the initial value of the investment.
e) Interest on interest accrued previously.

4. Why is diversification important?
a) To make investments more risky.
b) To concentrate investments in a single asset.
c) To reduce financial risk.
d) To increase the immediate profit potential.
e) To avoid long-term investments.

5. What is the most powerful factor of long-term investments?
a) Invest large amounts of money.
b) Time.
c) Invest only in shares.
d) Spend money on purchases.
e) Ignoring economic changes.

6. What does it mean to invest for the long term?
a) Invest for a short period, less than one year.
b) Invest for a moderate period, from 1 to 5 years.
c) Invest for a prolonged period, exceeding 5 years.
d) Invest only in shares.
e) Invest only in high-risk assets.

Answers

1) c
2) c
3) e
4) c
5) b
6) c

Marcelo Guerra

ACKNOWLEDGMENT

To those who have walked beside me on this journey, I would like to express my deepest gratitude. This book would not have been possible without the unwavering support and unconditional love **of my wife**, who has always been by my side, encouraging me and believing in me, even in times of doubt. His patience and understanding were instrumental in me being able to devote time to writing.

To my **children,** who fill my life with joy and inspiration, I want to thank them for being a constant source of motivation. Their laughter, their smiles, and their support have given me the strength to keep writing, even when the obstacles are insurmountable.

To my **friends**, who have been by my side throughout this process, sharing ideas, offering advice, and most of all, being a potential source of emotional support, my gratitude is endless. You have shown me that true friendship is a precious gift, and I am deeply grateful to have you in my life.
 I extend my thanks to the reviewers of this book, whose meticulous work and dedication helped polish my words and perfect my narrative. His ability to identify errors, suggest improvements, and ensure clarity of the text was invaluable to the final quality of this book.

To all of you, my gratitude is immense. This book is the result of a shared journey, and it is to you that I dedicate these pages. Thank you for being a part of my life and for making this dream a reality.

Marcelo Guerra

ABOUT THE AUTHOR

Solid academic background, has specialization in Business Management and specialization in Teaching in Professional Education. He worked as a teacher in technical and higher education courses. He is currently involved in the financial market and dedicates part of his time developing volunteer work.

www.ingramcontent.com/pod-product-compliance
Lightning Source LLC
Chambersburg PA
CBHW062335290526
45794CB00005B/2041